DELL 10¢ BOOK (repeating pattern)

A CAPTAIN DUNCAN MACLAIN MYSTERY

Author of
"Death Knell"
"The Iron Spiders"
"Blind Man's Bluff"

Cover Painting by Rafael de Soto

Published by DELL PUBLISHING COMPANY, INC.,
261 Fifth Avenue, New York 16, N. Y. George T. Delacorte, Jr., President;
Helen Meyer, Vice-President; Albert P. Delacorte, Vice-President. Designed
and produced by Western Printing & Lithographing Co. Printed in U.S.A.

About the Author . . . Just finishing his education at the time of World War I, Baynard Kendrick was the first American to volunteer for ■■■■■■ in the ■■■■dian

Kendrick made a th■■■■■ ■■■■■■■ ■■■ ways of the blind, gathering information which made him an invaluable instructor to blinded veterans during World War II. As a result of this experience he wrote a novel about an American blinded in the Italian campaign entitled *Lights Out.* Kendrick has also written a historical novel entitled *Flames of Time.* His first book, *Blood on Lake Louisa,* was published in 1934. Since then he has written many mysteries, among them are *The Last Express, Odor of Violets, Out of Control.*

The Murderer Who Wanted More

IT STARTED TO SNOW at half-past five in the afternoon. By nine, tiny stinging flakes beating against the casements of Bonnie Critten's Tenth Street apartment had ruled off the windows in sloping ridges of white.

Bonnie, looking much like a worried schoolgirl in the figure-hiding lines of her paint-stained smock, took a heavy overcoat from the closet and held it up for Captain Duncan Maclain. Under the weight of the overcoat, her hands were trembling.

"Add to my love of painting an imagination that works overtime," said Bonnie. "The man who knocked me on the head and robbed me was real enough. But this shooting at me out on Staten Island—" She paused, watching the set of the captain's neck above his well-tailored coat collar.

Duncan Maclain slid his strong arms into the overcoat and turned. For the briefest second, his perceptive fingers touched her own before they moved to clasp her hand.

"I've been blind for more than twenty years," he said, with a grin, "but even if you hadn't painted my dogs to advertise the glories of Porter's Dog Biscuits, I'd know you were an artist." His sightless eyes were fixed on the errant wave of her soft brown hair.

"What's artistic about me?" Bonnie laughed deprecatingly and made an attempt to smooth the offending hair. She had known Duncan Maclain for nearly a year and was still caught in those odd moments of confusion when she was certain he could see.

"Your fingers are a giveaway, Bonnie." He turned her hand palm up and gently smoothed the ball of her slender thumb. "You have remnants of paint and oil indelibly ground in here, and into two of your fingers as well. Infallible marks of the artist who works in oil."

"I might be a house painter," she protested.

The captain wrinkled his expressive nose. "There'd be a lurking odor of turpentine about you instead of perfume." He grew more serious as he released her hand. "I'm glad you asked me down here tonight, Bonnie. It's too bad I have to run along now, but Cappo is waiting downstairs with the car."

He raised his head to listen. "The wind must have hit fifty-five miles an hour. This is getting to be some storm."

"You don't think I'm being foolish, Captain? Worrying, I mean?" Bonnie's blue eyes darkened with sudden emotion as she returned to the subject foremost in her mind.

"I think you're a very brave and sensible woman," said Duncan Maclain. "To be attacked and knocked unconscious in one's own vestibule is no joke. Yet in three short weeks you're back at work again. When such an attack is followed by a close escape from an accidental shooting—" His broad shoulders shrugged expressively. "Suppose you stick close to your studio for a few days, Bonnie, while I go out to Staten Island and see what I can find. Good night."

He put his soft hat on and opened the door to the hall. Bonnie's studio was three flights up, but she made no offer to help him. A year of casual association had taught her that Duncan Maclain, in daylight or dark, was thoroughly capable of finding his way around.

She slipped out quietly after him and leaned over the railing to watch his tall, well-knit figure pursue its confident journey down. He walked with the sureness of previously counted steps, not deigning to touch the balustrade.

She returned to her apartment feeling a little awed. There was a quality of frightening perfection about Duncan Maclain. She knew he was engaged, but sometimes Bonnie wondered. Was Maclain's fiancée in love with the handsome, virile man, or fascinated by the cold perfection of a disembodied human machine?

The doorbell shrilled, three shorts and a long, before she had a chance to sit down. Bonnie answered eagerly, recognizing the welcome ring of her own fiancé, Alan Thorne. She felt the need of someone to talk to. Duncan Maclain, for all his quiet reserve, radiated so much pent-up animation that one felt enervated after his departure.

It was good to see Alan. He was a certified public accountant, competent, clearheaded, and not too talkative. Work in essential industry had temporarily postponed his induction, but notice of a pending commission had already come through.

His kiss was a tonic. Bonnie gave him a second for good measure. He held her off at arm's length, looking at the enveloping smock, then turned her quickly around.

"You look fourteen in that pinafore, darling. I think you've falsified your age as twenty-two." He smiled his crooked smile that made his narrow face so attractive.

"I've been entertaining a man," said Bonnie primly. "I have plenty of time to do that, waiting around up here for you."

"Um-m!" Alan grinned. "The big shot with the block-long car? We passed in the vestibule. What is it, more art work for you?"

"He's a detective, Alan. That's Captain Duncan Maclain. I used his dogs for the Porter ads. Remember?"

"Yes." Alan sat down and stretched his hands to the small cannel coal fire. "Maclain's been mixed up on some big jobs, Bonnie. He's clever as hell. What's he doing talking to you?"

"You mean I'm not so clever?" Bonnie turned her back and added a brush stroke to a painting on the easel.

"Don't be silly." Alan blew her a kiss. "And don't be difficult. Is he down here about that attack on you?"

"I asked him to come." Bonnie put down her brush and sat by Alan's feet on the floor. She lit a cigarette and stared at the fire. "Somebody took a shot at me last Saturday out in Tottenville, Alan."

He put out his hand and gently touched her wavy hair at the place where some marauder's blackjack had nearly fractured her skull. "Bonnie, why haven't you told me this before?"

"This is the first time I've seen you since I got back in town."

"And even now, I can't stay long," he said morosely. "I have to be back on another audit at ten. It will last until two certainly—income tax and the war. Tell me what happened to you."

"Maybe it was nothing." Bonnie smoked with short, consuming puffs. "I went out from Aunt Ludwina Vreeland's for a walk before dinner. You know how thick the woods are along Craig Avenue."

"The place of the Bad Woods," Alan quoted softly from the old Indian name. "Yes, Bonnie. Go on."

"Somebody took a shot at me from the woods. The bullet didn't miss me very far. It took a chunk from a tree not a foot away. I went back to the house on the run."

Bonnie bit her red lips and tossed the cigarette away. "Of course, it might not have been aimed at me, but coming after that mugging attempt three weeks ago—" Her slender shoulders drooped. "Alan, what would anyone want to kill me for?"

He bit thoughtfully at a thumbnail. "What did Captain Maclain have to say?"

"Nothing much. He told me to stay in for a while. He's going to do some investigating."

Alan said grimly, "Darling, so am I. I'm auditor for the Vreeland Estate, as you know. I haven't been over the accounts this year, but I'm starting tomorrow. You know very well your aunt's at the point of death."

"What has that to do with me?" Bonnie looked up.

"I don't know," said Alan, "but I'm going to try and find out." His narrow face was intense. "You were robbed by that man in the vestibule, weren't you?"

"Twenty-one dollars."

He nodded. "It's lucky the people on the ground floor heard your cry. Bonnie, I have to go." He stood up, raised her to her feet, and for an instant held her tight in his arms. "Do what Maclain says, Bonnie. If you have to go out, be careful crossing streets. If anything happened to you, I'd die."

Bonnie sat for some time contemplating the fire after Alan had gone. So many phases of her life had revolved around her Aunt Ludwina Vreeland's home. She could see it now: its storm-beaten walls turned brown, the jutting cubicle on its roof overlooking the windy sweep of land where Arthur Kill met Raritan Bay.

For all its historical significance, there was something about the gaunt Vreeland mansion that invariably depressed her; yet during most of her childhood, and even more since her mother's death three years before, Bonnie had considered it as home.

She had explored its tangled grounds with her three cousins, Fred, De Frees, and Katherine—an inseparable quartet of youthful pirates launching miniature warships on the banks of Arthur Kill, Katherine always in command.

Fred was an affectionate swaggerer, living in a play to cover a sensitivity that had turned him into a drunkard as the years moved on. De Frees was the diplomat, gently soothing even at the age of ten, the patcher-up of childhood quarrels usually engendered by demonstrations of Katherine's inflexible will.

Even with Aunt Ludwina—a proud, cantankerous woman, shy of humor and possessed of a firm Dutch jaw—De Frees by sheer blandishment managed to get his own way. To Bonnie, he was the most lovable of them all. Fred was sweet, but weak.

Katherine was pleasant and highly polished, but her life revolved around herself and no one else. To Katherine; other people's problems were annoyances to be firmly dismissed. Her relationship with Bonnie was honeyed. Deep down, both of them knew that they could never be real friends. Bonnie had too much character to agree unreservedly with everything Katherine Vreeland had to say.

Bonnie shook off her retrospective mood with an effort and went to her easel. A painting of a round-eyed baby, snapshotted in Washington Square a week before, was due to be shown to Conger's advertising agency in the morning.

She worked until midnight, then put down her brush and stepped back from the easel, with an uncomfortable realization that the heat had quit a couple of hours before. The cannel coal fire in the small iron grate had died to a few pale embers.

Her hands were cold as she mechanically cleaned her brushes with turpentine, washed them out in soap and water, and stood them up in a jar. From the canvas, the baby watched her routine suspiciously with a sidelong glance. She was just finishing when the telephone rang.

"Miss Critten?"

"Yes." Bonnie perched on the arm of a chair, drawing a flannel dressing-gown closer about her.

"This is Dr. Satterlee—"

"Oh!" It took an instant for Bonnie to place the doctor in his proper niche. "Something's happened to Aunt Ludwina?" she managed to say.

"Not yet." The physician's incisive voice remained professionally cool. "But Mrs. Vreeland, as you know, has been quite ill."

"I was out there last week-end."

"She's had a turn for the worse tonight."

"Is there anything I can do?" asked Bonnie, not seeing how there really could be.

"I'm phoning from Tottenville," Satterlee told her impatiently. "Mrs. Vreeland would like to talk with you."

"On the phone?"

"I'm afraid she's scarcely able to use the phone, Bonnie." The doctor's voice was dry. "Perhaps I didn't make it quite clear that your aunt's about to die."

"I'll come first thing in the morning, Dr. Satterlee."

"You'll arrive in ample time for the funeral, Bonnie." Wind battered disturbingly against the panes, piling up more snow. "If you hurry, you can catch a ferry at half-past one. It connects with the late train at one fifty-nine. I'll meet you in Tottenville."

"Of course," said Bonnie numbly. The baby in her painting was eyeing her with increased suspicion as she hung up the phone. She addressed it irritably: "Don't stare at me as if I were crazy! What else can I do?"

Dressing took interminably long. Galoshes were missing, as usual. Two minutes of rooting in the closet failed to produce them. Bonnie was horribly sleepy and her brain wasn't functioning at its best. Finally, under the spur of determined concentration she remembered that she'd left them outside in the hall. She closed the apartment door, and sat down on the top steps to tug the overshoes on.

A late party broke up in one of the apartments below with a chorus of laughing good nights. Bonnie waited until the guests departed. With such an outburst of merriment going on it was most unlikely that another holdup man would be lingering in the downstairs vestibule. A few minutes later, when she let herself out onto Tenth Street, the laughing guests had vanished into the storm.

Wind-driven ice water smashed at her with the force of a boxer's blow. She gave one hopeless glance down the street in search of a taxi, then plowed grimly along in the direction of the subway station.

Frightful nervousness quickened her steps, but the effort of walking was dreamlike and disturbing. There were moments when her head still ached from the blow of three weeks before. New York had been fighting an epidemic of mugging—the Harlem term for robbery with violence—and Bonnie's experience had been one of many. That made it no less frightening. Now she ruthlessly put down a desire to look back over her shoulder. She was sure that there were footsteps behind her, automatically growing closer with each concealing blast of wind.

She had always scoffed at woman's instinct, but hers was working overtime right now. Was somebody methodically stalking her through the storm? Panic struck her, but her frozen muscles refused to respond.

Twin lights swung slowly into the dark street, and a cruising police car crawled by. Bonnie breathed a sigh of relief. Blood pounded exultantly through her, warding off a threatened chill. She found her hand on the rail of the subway steps and clutched it tight to keep from stumbling down.

The attendant in the booth looked up from a magazine as he changed her quarter. "You look plenty cold."

"And how," said Bonnie. Her eyes were on the entrance stairs. A man in a sleet-caked black overcoat, belted close at the waist, was coming down. He swept one swift, hard glance over Bonnie's fur coat and dropped a nickel in the turnstile slot. She waited a few seconds before following. It was silly, but she had a frightful sensation of being caught in a game she didn't know how to play.

She descended slowly to the train level and found the platform deserted. At the foot of the stairs Bonnie paused and looked it up and down. The very absence of bustle and roar was disquieting. She moved forward, her rubber-soled feet making no sound.

Stark metal pillars, evenly spaced—man-made stalactites. Trickling water, carrying tiny pieces of rubbish sluggishly along a miniature creek between shining rails.

The man in the belted coat had vanished.

Bonnie stepped closer to the edge of the tracks and peered northward up the long, dark tunnel. There were no colored lights in sight to mark the welcome approach of a train.

When she straightened up the man was standing close beside her. She realized then that he had been concealed from her view by the darkened newsstand at the center of the platform.

He said nothing and made no move to come closer, yet Bonnie felt paralyzed under his impersonal, calculating stare. Flat black eyes measured her out of a chalky face. Trivial details began to impress her—the excellent cut of his overcoat, the gnarled knuckles of his idly hanging hands, the streak of gray in his hair.

Behind her a masculine voice said, "Bonnie!" She pivoted quickly. Carl Raecke, a shipbuilder from Staten Island, was smiling and holding out his hand.

"Carl," she said. "Oh, Carl—"

The man in the belted coat moved away. Raecke studied her gravely, hanging on to her hand. "What's the matter? Did I give you a scare?"

"No. I already had the scare. Sheer nerves." She told him about the doctor's telephone call. "I thought that someone was following me—that man over there."

Raecke's pleasant, square face clouded. "Did he—?"

Bonnie smiled. "He didn't do anything except look at me quite impersonally." Composure was returning. The world was normal again, restored by the magic of a middle-aged businessman holding protectively to her arm. There was safety in his smile, refuge from the unknown in his cultured voice.

A train rattled in. The cars weren't full, but she sat unnecessarily close to Carl. Doors slammed and the train moved out.

"I'm sorry about Ludwina," he said above the din. "You're her niece, aren't you?"

Bonnie nodded. "She hasn't been well for quite a long time."

He looked disapproving. "This is a hell of a night to

drag a kid like you out to Tottenville. Was that Satterlee's idea?"

"Aunt Ludwina wanted to talk to me. She may not live out the night."

"I'm going as far as Dongan Hills. If you're nervous, I'll be glad to ride on with you to Tottenville."

"Certainly not," Bonnie refused firmly. "Dr. Satterlee's going to meet me."

"Suppose he doesn't?" Raecke wasn't satisfied. "Suppose he's held up by this storm?"

"Then I'll have to find a taxi—or they'll have a guest for the night in the station waiting-room at Tottenville."

"I don't like it, Bonnie," he blurted out. "Weren't you robbed about a month ago?"

She nodded, smiling. "I'm trying to forget it. But, frankly, I feel much better since you happened along."

Raecke took a look down the car, as though he might locate the white-faced man. Then he smiled down at Bonnie. "You're an artist, aren't you? Ludwina, or somebody, told me you were doing quite well. I've sort of lost track of you since you've grown. You're not married, are you?"

"Engaged. A boy named Alan Thorne."

"I haven't seen Ludwina in a couple of years. I suppose she's still in the old Vreeland mansion on the hill."

"Nobody could move her—except death, probably." Bonnie sighed.

"You never liked it as a child, as I recall."

"Ugh!" Bonnie shivered. "I don't like it today."

"Still, it's quite historical," he reminded her. "Next to Captain Billopp's it's one of the oldest on the island."

"Too historical," Bonnie agreed musingly. "Places with guaranteed ghosts and certified dungeons make me slightly ill."

Carl Raecke laughed. "Future generations will probably visit it as a museum. Schoolteachers will haul the kids in and point out bloodstains on the slave quarters' floor."

"I've always suspected my practical cousin Katherine of keeping those stains in good repair," Bonnie admitted. "When new visitors arrive, nice, two-hundred-year-old bloodstains are something to show."

They got out at South Ferry and dashed up to the street with just a few minutes to spare. At the top they halted for a second, checked by the cutting force of the snow, whipped onto the Battery from across New York Bay. Bonnie covered the short distance from subway station to ferryhouse clinging to Carl Raecke's arm, her head bent low.

The ferry was already in the slip, and the warmth of the vast saloon on the upper deck struck delightfully against Bonnie's freezing body, enfolding her in.

"God, this feels good!" Raecke exclaimed, loosening his coat and ridding himself of melting snow.

Bonnie huddled silently into a corner by a window and stared out into the blackness. Powerful engines began their rhythmic thrum. Far off on the water a deep-throated whistle bellowed. The ferry moved ponderously out, and instantly the Manhattan shore was lost from sight.

Raecke glanced at Bonnie once before busying himself with an evening paper. Unconscious of being rude to her escort, Bonnie kept her face toward the window. Twice she had been abroad, but somehow Europe and England had never impressed her as being so remote from New York as Staten Island just across the bay. It was the names, she decided, that lent the island its magnified sense of distance: Arthur Kill. Kill van Kull. Great Fresh Kill. Such names brought pictures of dikes and turning windmills, of wooden shoes and tulip time. They had no place adjacent to the stark modernity of New York.

Out of the black a flashing green light winked through the snow at Bonnie's musings. With it came the doleful sound of a bell.

When the ferry docked, Bonnie and Raecke hurried

into the rear car of the two-car Tottenville local train. Forty minutes of comparative comfort, then Bonnie knew she would face the full rigors of the weather. Tottenville, at the southern end of the island and unprotected from the sea, would be sure to catch it all.

The train moved off. Raecke was tenderly rolling his unlighted cigar.

"I was thinking about the Vreeland mansion, Bonnie."

"Again?"

He nodded, staring at the cigar—a thoughtful man, Raecke, well fed, using words with care. Yet Bonnie felt his calmness concealed a worried air. "She's kept it up so consistently." He paused and moved uncomfortably under the frankness of Bonnie's stare. "Maybe it's out of place to bring this up right now, but I can't help wondering who'll inherit your aunt's house when she's gone."

"Katherine most likely, or maybe De Frees."

The small pouches under Raecke's eyes showed wrinkles. "Isn't there another son?"

"Fred," said Bonnie, and stopped.

"Oh, yes, I remember—" Raecke pocketed his cigar.

"Everybody probably remembers," Bonnie remarked after a moment. "He's been a heavy drinker for a long time and been in more than one jam. Yet, when I was a kid, he was always my favorite. Kindly but weak, I guess."

"Yes," said Raecke. "Those fellows so often are."

The train was coming into a station. Raecke's pale eyes flickered toward the exit. Suddenly, without a word, he raised his hat and slipped from the car, a second ahead of the closing door.

Bonnie started to call, "This isn't Dongan Hills!" but it was far too late. She leaned back in her seat. Queer that a man could miss his own station when he'd lived in a place so long!

The train moved slowly on, while Bonnie dozed. Some time later she sat up with a jerk. Nervously she realized that she was the last passenger left in the car. She moved up closer to the conductor.

He asked in friendly fashion, "Tottenville?"

Bonnie nodded.

"Not many tonight," he said. "One drunk in the other car and you. That's all."

Although no passengers were getting off at Atlantic Station, the last before Tottenville, the sliding doors opened, nevertheless, to admit a blast of wet, spiraling snow which whirled across the platform of the car. Then the doors slid shut.

Bonnie sat erect, alert and startled. Just as the train began to move she had heard two sharp reports above the rushing wind. They were spaced so close that they almost blended. The noise seemed to come from the front of the train.

The conductor sat down.

"Trucks backfiring—or a bus, maybe," he exclaimed. "Arthur Kill Road runs close to the tracks at Atlantic Station."

Bonnie left her seat, walked to the vestibule, and stood looking into the forward car.

"Your drunk has fallen off the seat," she told the conductor. "At least, his feet are sticking out into the aisle."

"He's a nuisance." The conductor got up and pushed past her. "One of the Vreelands."

"Oh!" Bonnie put a hand to her breast. "They're cousins of mine." She followed the conductor down the aisle.

Fred Vreeland's light gray hat had fallen off. Its owner was stretched out face down. Bonnie clutched dizzily at a handle on one of the seat backs.

The conductor bent over, then straightened up slowly, staring unbelievingly at the red stain on his fingers. "Now, what the hell!" he muttered. "That guy's not drunk. He's dead!"

The window by the right-hand front seat was shattered.

Already the place where Fred Vreeland had sat was wet with a tiny mound of melting snow.

Dr. Satterlee, gauntly professional, said, "It's Fred Vreeland. I can identify him positively."

It was half an hour later. The train had arrived in the Tottenville station, where the doctor was waiting for Bonnie. Now the police, in the person of Patrolman Burke, had arrived and taken over.

The patrolman was very busily asking questions and putting down answers in a notebook. When it came her turn, Bonnie found herself mumbling her name and address through lips that were frostily numb.

"Why were you coming to Tottenville?" Burke asked.

"My aunt, Mrs. Ludwina Vreeland, is dying."

"Did you have to wait for so late a train?"

"Dr. Satterlee just phoned me a little while ago."

"Then you and Fred Vreeland were together?"

"No."

"No?"

"I didn't even know he was on the train."

"Then how did you happen to find him?"

"The conductor found him—that is, I just saw that he'd fallen on the floor."

"But you knew he was your cousin?"

"Not until the conductor told me he was one of the Vreelands."

"You didn't know, but the conductor did. Now, lady—"

"I just saw his feet sticking out in the aisle. I was standing in the vestibule."

"Why were you looking into the front car?"

Bonnie's breath kept catching in her throat. "Why does one do those things? I don't know. Do you?"

"No, ma'am," said Patrolman Burke, and wrote something down. Then, to Satterlee: "She says you called her. Is that true?"

"This is preposterous!" The doctor blew his long, red

nose with fervor. His eyes were watering. To Bonnie, his lips looked blue. "Certainly it's true. I told her I'd meet her here. What do you think I came to the station for?"

"Maybe to meet the dead man," said Burke. "Didn't you telephone him, too?"

"No." Dr. Satterlee took a tissue from his overcoat pocket, cleaned moisture from his glasses, and put them back on.

"Why not?" asked Burke. "Why did you call Miss Critten, and not call Mrs. Vreeland's own son?"

"Because Mrs. Vreeland is dying. She asked to see her niece, but she didn't ask to see her son."

"That's screwy," said Patrolman Burke. "My mother wanted to see me before she died."

"I congratulate you," the doctor remarked dryly. He cleaned his glasses again, his surgeon's fingers working busily. "You are probably a sober, industrious young man."

"And this fellow?" Burke eyed Satterlee suspiciously and pointed toward the body with his thumb.

"He was a dipsomaniac, among other things."

"Oh," said Burke. "A stew."

"And how," the conductor put in.

The patrolman scowled him into silence. "I'm coming to you." He returned to Satterlee. "Somebody must 'a' tipped him off his mother was dying. Who was it, if it wasn't you?"

"I'm sure I don't know. I'll try to find out if it will be of help to you."

"We'll find out," Burke declared. He faced the conductor. "Now you. How did you know who this guy was—and that he was a stew?"

"I ain't blind, Burke." The conductor winked at the motorman. "I been riding this line for years. You learn a lot about Staten Island people and what they do. Now, this young lady wasn't with her cousin—like she's been tellin' you. She got on with Mr. Raecke at St. George, and he got off at Old Town. He usually goes to Dongan

Hills. Maybe he was drinkin', too."

Satterlee's eyes moved to Bonnie. "Carl Raecke? Is that true?"

"Yes," she explained quickly.

The doctor studied her drawn face. "If Miss Critten is to talk with her aunt, I must get her to the house without delay. You can find us there in the morning, Officer."

"Well, I suppose—" Burke began doubtfully.

"Thank you." Satterlee was decisive. He took Bonnie's arm. His grip was tight to a point of painfulness as he steered her past the few late watchers and down the ramp to the street.

There the feeble, spongy lights fought helplessly against a great, white screen swept across the waters of Arthur Kill. Bonnie dared one swift glance out over the water in the direction of the New Jersey shore. Then, blinded by stinging flakes, she lowered her head again and let Satterlee lead her to his car.

Chilled and miserable, neither of them spoke during the drive to the ancient house where Ludwina Vreeland lay dying. When the car stopped, Bonnie peered out. A shaded window made a single misty patch a story above the ground, throwing into black relief four great pillars. Lower, in the recess of the pillared porch, a fanlight marked the door.

Bonnie said, "Are you going to tell her? About Fred, I mean."

"Not if I can help it. What's the use?" Satterlee reached across her and opened the door.

Bonnie got out, clutching her week-end bag, and they crossed the wind-swept porch together.

Satterlee said, "I left the front door unlocked when I went to meet you."

Inside, a stairway curved upward from the great front hall. The dying embers of a huge log fire glowed blood-red on copper pitchers flanking the open hearth. Bonnie moved closer to the mantel without removing her furs.

The doctor took off his coat and hung it up in a closet after shaking loose the snow.

Upstairs someone started to moan. The sound trickled down the staircase, sounding scarcely human—a whimpering staccato, overwhelmingly grief-stricken, disturbingly penetrating and low.

Satterlee said, "That sounds like Oroondates. Ludwina would have a damned old fool of a butler. He's been stoking up with gin all day."

A woman in a white, starched uniform floated part way down the staircase and peered over the railing into the hall. She saw Satterlee and beckoned.

The doctor lit a cigarette and ran lightly up after her. A few minutes later he came back down.

Bonnie was still in front of the fireplace. Satterlee didn't look at her.

"I could have saved you the trip," he said, and tossed the butt of his cigarette into the fire. "She died five minutes ago." He shrugged. "Maybe it's better. Fred's murder was something of a problem, after all."

The sobbing ceased as suddenly as it had begun. Bonnie's head turned toward the staircase. Her cousin, De Frees, was coming down. He wore a heavy black dressing-gown trimmed in vivid scarlet and had thrust his small feet into leather sandals which flapped softly against each step. In spite of his disheveled dark hair, beginning to recede from his high, smooth forehead, and the informality of his attire, he still managed to retain an air of being exceptionally well groomed.

"Hello, Bonnie." De Frees's regular white teeth flashed a grin at her which momentarily eased the somberness of the room. "Why don't you take off your things and stay a while? Or is it cold in here?" He crossed to the fireplace and put the back of his well-kept hand against her cheek. "You're cold, at any rate." He took a heavy log from the hearth and dumped it with a crash onto the dying fire.

Sparks flew up.

Satterlee, his hands clasped behind him, was standing, rigid as a soldier, watching De Frees. He said, with a shade of rebuke, "Your mother died a few minutes ago."

"Could I miss, with Oroondates holding a crying jag outside my bedroom door?" De Frees took a Cape Cod lighter from its polished brass receptacle and touched a match to it. He thrust the flaming lighter under the log and straightened up. "Take off your furs, Bonnie. It will soon be warm."

Bonnie walked slowly to the closet, slipped out of her coat, and put it on a hanger.

The log crackled fitfully and began to burn.

"Where's Katherine?" asked Satterlee.

"Up, I think. I heard her moving about in her room. She'd stop to dress properly at the crack of doom." De Frees vanished into the dark square of the dining-room and came back with a small glass of brandy. "Drink this, Bonnie. You look as if you need it."

Bonnie said, "Thanks, De Frees. I do," and gulped some.

"That's better." De Frees smiled. "I thought the cat had got your tongue."

"Bonnie's upset," said Satterlee. "More so than you."

"That's your fault," said De Frees shortly. "It was idiotic dragging her out here at this time of night, and in a storm." He flopped into a chair, and then was up again instantly. "I'd better call the undertaker and get it over. Funerals are barbarous. They depress me."

"You'll have two, unfortunately," said Satterlee.

"What do you mean by that, Dr. Satterlee?" Katherine Vreeland's warm contralto asked the question from the staircase.

Bonnie ran up to greet her. It was queer what unimportant items could take possession of the mind. Even as Katherine kissed her, Bonnie found herself thinking that De Frees had been right.

Katherine's heavy black hair was brushed and rolled

with artistic precision. Her angular body was draped to perfection in a tailored suit of brown. Wide-set, sympathetic eyes of dark gray, a fine, straight nose, and a mouth touched with humor kept her from being severe.

At the foot of the stairs she swept a quick glance about the dancing shadows of the hall. "Where's Fred?" she asked.

Satterlee thrust forward a chair with an air of desperation. "Katherine, please sit down."

"What's happened to him now?" Katherine's words were impelling by their softness. She ignored the chair.

"He was killed on the train." Satterlee began a nervous pacing, feeling his mouth with gentle fingers as though he might be covering some disfiguring scar.

"Killed?" said De Frees. "That's insane!" The firelight touched wrinkles, making him look suddenly old and withered. "How could Fred get killed on the train?"

"He was shot."

"But—" Katherine broke off on the single word, a word that was full of sorrow and sharp with pain. She looked at Bonnie for confirmation, and back at the doctor again.

"Through the window, somehow. Maybe some soldiers on night maneuvers. Maybe—" Satterlee stumbled badly in his effort to explain.

Katherine Vreeland's face set into a classic mask. "Mother and Fred in an hour. . . . Were you with him, Bonnie?"

"No." Bonnie felt as though some powerful mental anesthetic were seeping into her brain. This whole frightful cycle might go on forever: "Were you with him, Bonnie?" "No!" she'd keep saying, but her story would have to be told again and again.

Satterlee came to her rescue. "I can tell you what happened, Katherine—that is, all we know for the moment. Right now I want to get Bonnie to bed before I have another patient on my hands."

"Of course," agreed Katherine dully. "I sent Oroondates and Wilma to their room, Bonnie. If you can make out for yourself, go on up. Take the big guest room. If you need anything you can rifle my bureau."

"I brought a week-end bag," Bonnie said gratefully. "It's there by the door."

Katherine reached out with a sudden impulsive gesture and took her hand. "I'd come up with you, but I have to hear what happened. Have you anything to make you sleep?"

"No." Bonnie kissed her lightly. "I'll be okay."

As she started upstairs Satterlee handed her a tiny tin box. "Take one of these. It will quiet you."

The upstairs hall was dim. Bonnie paused at the top of the stairs. A door opened softly. She saw the nurse look out. The door closed again.

She could hear Katherine's voice from downstairs: "I might as well have killed him. I'm responsible for his being on that train."

Bonnie found a table lamp in the guest room and switched it on. The radiance beat feebly against an ancient parchment shade of ugly brown. The little light that managed to escape soaked itself into tapestried walls and brought into being the four knurled posts of the mammoth canopied bedstead.

The room was cold.

Bonnie touched the satin bedspread and drew her fingers away. Its sleek surface was overlaid with the frigidity of long disuse. It felt coated with the permanent ice of death. She shuddered.

Death had struck twice at the Vreeland family since midnight. Aunt Ludwina's had been expected. Aunt Ludwina was old. But Fred—Fred had never harmed anyone but himself. She'd miss him terribly, yet that wasn't all. The bullet fired from the trees on the previous Saturday had come singingly alive in the short time since Fred's murder.

Death had struck at the Vreelands before. If tradition

was to be believed, one Ludwig Vreeland had been stabbed to death while sadistically flogging a slave girl. His blood still stained the floor of the quarters over the room where Bonnie was right now.

She was sorry she remembered that. It brought back a picture of Fred again—dead on the floor of the train.

Bonnie opened her week-end bag and hustled into her nightgown and flannel dressing-gown.

A board creaked sharply.

She stood still, her hands clenched firmly, her soft chin set tight with a listening line. She knew the sound of that creaking board. The slave quarters were above her. A narrow, dark stairway, long unused, led up to them from the kitchen below.

The creaking board was on the landing, where a door opened out to the second-floor hall. Bonnie had led the neighbors' children on too many scary journeys up and down that stairway not to know. She had frightened Aunt Ludwina so many times by popping unexpectedly into the hall that the door on the landing had been fixed securely with two large screws at least ten years before.

Wind shrieked over Arthur Kill, rattling the windows and piling up more snow. Bonnie knew her nerves had finally snapped. The ghost of Ludwig Vreeland, stabbed by a pain-crazed slave girl, climbed those stairs on windy nights with footsteps staid and slow.

She went to the bed and sat down. Her hand reached out for the box of Satterlee's sleeping-capsules—five of them packed like sardines in the small container. Five comfortable, dreamless nights for the wakeful, laid out in a single row.

Drowsy reaction seized her. The capsules could wait. If she couldn't sleep, reading a while might help. She put the box on the table beside her, added a book from her suitcase, then, toothbrush in hand, sought the bathroom at the other end of the hall.

The talking downstairs had ceased, but a quiet muttering came from behind the door of Aunt Ludwina's room.

Bonnie brought a glass of water back to the guest room with her. She put it on the bedside table, threw back the icy covers, and slid between the sheets without removing her dressing-gown. With the light out, she lay on her back, trying to calculate the bulk of the canopy above her.

Down in the house a noisy, whirring clock struck five.

Her brain was racing, to no purpose—running her around a horrible track of danger. She had known before she switched off the light that something had changed.

Something, she knew, had been altered during the short time she was absent from the room.

Staring up at the formless canopy, Bonnie retraced her entry into the room.

Holding the glass of water, she had closed the door, gone to the table, and put the water down beside the book.

She reached out of bed for the table lamp and turned it back on. It struck brightly into her dilated pupils and for seconds she couldn't see. Then, like a quickly focused picture, the jacket of the current mystery she'd brought with her stood out in all its vivid color.

Bonnie leaned on her elbow, staring. The front of the jacket was upward, but it hadn't been when she put the book on the table. There was a picture of the author on the back. She'd looked at it just before she got her tooth-brush—looked at it after the book was on the table. The features of the author were in her mind right now. Someone had turned the book over while she was out of the room. That much was forcefully stark and clear.

She slumped down in the bed again. Katherine, of course. She'd dropped in while Bonnie was out, picked up the book, and put it down again.

Bonnie Critten needed a capsule. She had reached the stage where the most normal of happenings seemed queer.

She moved the book, which was covering the little tin box, slid back the lid, and dumped a capsule into her palm.

Funny what shattered nerves could do! The capsules had been bright yellow when Bonnie first saw them, bright yellow before her trip to the bathroom down the hall. Now her imagination made them look almost light brown.

Well, it was almost morning, anyway. She put the capsule back in the box and lay down. . . .

When she awoke, Wilma was standing beside her bed holding an invalid's tray. Wilma was gray-haired and wrinkled. Aunt Ludmina had liked to refer to her as "my housekeeper"—a term glorifying the harassed maid of all work.

Oroondates, her husband, frailer than his wife, had been beaten down by his multifarious duties years before, and now took to the surreptitious stimulus of schnapps. Wilma's face and hands reflected her lengthy drudgery, but her body was still straight and tall.

"The snow's stopped," said Wilma, "but the day's gray and it's like to start again." She spoke with a slow-spaced rhythm, reminiscent of an accent that Bonnie had never quite been able to fathom. Oroondates spoke perfect English, but his background was as Dutch as a dike.

"Wilma, you're a darling." Bonnie sat up in bed. A log was blazing in the fireplace. Some of the room's unpleasant chill had fled. "Did you start that fire, too?"

"Oroondates." Wilma placed the tray of gleaming service across Bonnie's knees. "He's a mouse."

"He must be. I didn't hear him at all." Bonnie squinted at the tray with a suspicious frown. "Wilma, isn't that Aunt Ludwina's invalid tray?"

"She'd like you to use it—if she knew." Wilma gave a leathery smile. "Oroondates got it from the bedroom while the nurse was out." Wilma stopped at the door. "It's past eleven. Miss Katherine asked will you hurry a little. There are men here to see you."

"What men?"

"There were a lot of reporters. Now they're gone, and

the lawyer's here."

"Mr. Hedges?" Bonnie's lips pursed, as though the orange juice had suddenly turned sour. "You said men, Wilma."

"There's more. Police, I think." Wilma opened the door. "A queer lot, for sure. Inspector Davis is one."

The memory of Fred's death rushed back at Bonnie, effectually to ruin her breakfast.

"Are there more?" asked Bonnie, poking a piece of toast with a listless finger.

"There are," said Wilma, quietly triumphant. "One brought dogs."

"Dogs?" Bonnie looked up quickly.

"Two big dogs." Wilma's wrinkled lips set in disapproval. "And one of them in harness." She stared at Bonnie, hoping for a question.

Bonnie stared back.

"He's blind," said Wilma. She went outside, with that, and closed the door.

So Captain Duncan Maclain had arrived!

Bonnie smoked a cigarette with her coffee, then put the tray aside. Out of bed, she paused in dressing and stood staring at the bleakness outside the window.

The air had cleared. Beyond the white slope from the Vreeland house, a tanker slid silently along the Kill. She decided she preferred the howling wind of the night before. Staten Island today was as white and formless as a winding sheet. Its air was too clean. Its heart was too frighteningly still.

"Nonsense," she said, and tugged her stockings on. When she went downstairs there was a defiant, arrogant set to her firm chin.

Katherine was presiding, ruling a circle about the fireplace—a tailored hostess who seemed to have stepped intact from some Fifth Avenue window. *Sleek as any wax model*, thought Bonnie, *and just as cool.*

Or was she just as cool? By her chair, ashes from her

cigarette had made gray patches on the polished floor.

The three men stood up as Bonnie reached the bottom step.

Bruce Hedges, the lawyer, said, "Bonnie, my dear child, it's delightful to see you again." The blazing fire flickered against the distinguished white at his temples. He was legal efficiency at its zenith.

Bonnie tried to keep distaste from her voice. "How are you, Mr. Hedges?" He was old enough to be her father. Since she was fifteen she'd dodged being left alone with him in a room. He had no right to call her "my dear child." She hesitated now as he bustled forward to greet her, sensing in advance the provoking pressure of his fingers on her arm.

"Hello, Bonnie! We didn't think you were coming down at all." Hedges was eased aside by the tall, immaculate form of Duncan Maclain. The cut-in was accomplished with such easy fluidity and such finesse that Bonnie scarcely knew how it happened.

One second she was expecting Hedges. The next, her hand was safe in the strong, assuring clasp of the fast-moving captain. Relief surged through her. She fell in step beside him, glad to have him escort her across the room.

"This is Inspector Larry Davis, of the New York Homicide Squad," the captain said. "Bonnie and I are quite old friends."

Davis shook her hand. His graying mustache was neat and well trimmed. His clothes were those of a prosperous merchant. A spark of friendship glowed in his steel-gray eyes. Back of it all, Bonnie felt herself the subject of a searching mind which had put her in a card file labeled "Critten, B. Female. White. 22."

Everything friendly and casual, nothing grim. Tension back of it all.

Bonnie sat down. Captain Maclain eased himself into an armchair. Bonnie stared at the German shepherd dogs

—one on each side of him—eyeing her phlegmatically with upward glances from the floor. Even when she'd painted them, they had remained self-sufficient, ready to accept her on the captain's say-so—that and no more.

A car drew up outside. The captain broke off abruptly and leaned back. De Frees and Dr. Satterlee came in, stamping off snow.

"Well," said De Frees, with a look around, "I see that the party's still on. . . . Hello, Bonnie. Who dug you out of bed?"

Satterlee squirmed out of his coat. "We've arranged for funeral services."

The inspector's heavy brows moved a fraction closer. "We came out together, but our missions are slightly different." He went to perch himself on the edge of an antique table, with astonishing overconfidence in the skill of its maker. "Frankly, Captain Maclain was brought here by the death of Mrs. Vreeland."

Satterlee looked up from filling a pipe, and Bonnie watched a few grains of yellow tobacco trickle to the floor. "Mrs. Vreeland died a natural death. I've already signed a certificate to that effect. Miss Waterman, a registered nurse, has been with her for four months or longer. I've been attending her for some time. Her body was removed to the undertaker's early this morning."

"So I understand," said Davis.

"I'm afraid *I* don't understand a lot of things." Dr. Satterlee examined Maclain over a match flame. "Captain Maclain is a private investigator of some reputation. His interest in the natural death of one of my patients is—"

"I'm not so much interested in her death," said Maclain. "I'm interested in the property she left."

Bruce Hedges had been sitting in a high-backed chair letting his opaque eyes move from speaker to speaker. He asked a question now, using his spatulate fingers to smooth down one side of his hair. "Any specific property, Captain Maclain?"

"For the moment, I'm not at liberty to say."

"Then I don't see how I can be of help. Her holdings were extensive."

"You can be of help by revealing as soon as possible the terms of Ludwina Vreeland's will." The captain was silkily friendly.

"That's rather a family matter."

"Don't be stuffy, Bruce," said Katherine. "The family's all here now. Certainly, I have no objection. De Frees?"

"Personally," said her brother, "I'd be glad to hear what she had to say."

"I consider such a proceeding unwise." Hedges glanced at his watch and put it away.

"Why?" asked Davis.

The lawyer's uncompromising lips set tightly. "A will is a family matter, after all."

"The terms of this one will hit the newspapers sooner or later," said Davis smoothly. "The quicker I hear them, the sooner I may put a murderer back of the bars."

De Frees looked up. "What could Fred's murder have to do with a will? Mother wasn't dead."

"She was dying," said Davis, with a scowl.

"Your remark seems gratuitous, Inspector," Hedges put in. "Such an assumption directly points suspicion at a legatee."

"I'm suspicious of everyone when bodies begin to fall."

"You didn't know Fred Vreeland very well." Hedges was disapprovingly grim. "I'd be inclined to search for a distraught woman who—"

"What, Bruce?" Bonnie sensed venom back of De Frees's inquiring grin. "Let's say that Fred's personal life was his own. You never approved of him while he was alive. Anything you say can only be conjecture, now that he's gone."

"I agree." Katherine smoothed her tailored skirt down over one knee. "Suppose, Bruce, that you read the will."

"Very well," said Hedges with an overtone of surliness. He went to the closet for a shiny briefcase and brought it back to his chair. A tiny key unlocked it. A zipper purred. Papers crackled louder than the fire.

"It was drawn three months ago—dictated to my stenographer in Mrs. Vreeland's room while I was present. . . . *I, Ludwina Vreeland, being of sound mind—*"

"If any of you are interested," said Duncan Maclain from the depths of his chair, "somebody is listening at the top of the stairs."

De Frees bounced from his seat and went up two steps at a time. He was back in a moment with Oroondates in tow. The bent, white-haired old butler stared unabashed from reddened eyes at the solemn assembly.

"She'd want me to hear," he announced in a voice slightly quavery. "She's left money to me and Wilma, we know."

"You're drunk again," Katherine told him. Her tone wasn't harsh, but her face clouded with a frown.

"A drop only, Miss Katherine." Oroondates bowed with a formal unsteadiness. "My sorrow's too deep to drown."

"He's in the will for a small amount." Hedges rustled the heavy bond paper. "Let him stay."

"Take that chair in the corner, Oroondates," De Frees ordered curtly, "and stay sitting down."

"*—to my beloved daughter, Katherine, one hundred thousand dollars—*

"*—to my son, De Frees, fifty thousand dollars, and in addition the Vreeland house and all my Staten Island . . .*

"*—to my son, Frederick, ten thousand dollars, and in addition a trust fund sufficient to assure him an income for the remainder of his life of thirty-six hundred dollars per year.*

"*—to my devoted niece, Bonnie Critten—*"

Hedges coughed.

Bonnie found that her hands were clasped so tightly

that her fingers were tingling. A suffocating air of waiting had blanketed the room.

"—to my devoted niece, Bonnie Critten, ten thousand dollars; and should she survive her cousin, Frederick Vreeland, the trust fund established for his life shall, in turn, revert to her. Upon her death, said trust fund shall become the property of the Pleasant Plains Hospital, a corporation, to use as it may see fit—"

"Does that mean that Bonnie gets Fred's trust fund now?" asked Katherine.

"Precisely." Hedges kept his eyes on the paper.

"I'm glad," said Katherine, with a smile.

"—to my faithful servants, Oroondates and Wilma Maury, who have served me so long, five thousand dollars each, and my house in St. Petersburg, Florida . . .

"—to my counselor and friend, Bruce Hedges, ten thousand dollars, in addition to the regular administration fee . . ."

Hedges' unctuous voice went on and on. There were meaningless details endlessly prolonged. Bonnie felt herself drawn to the blind man slumped in his chair, held to him by some sympathetic bond, as though both of them were present, and still outside of it all.

Fred Vreeland's life income was hers—because Fred was dead, because Fred had been murdered.

Satterlee was talking. "Do I understand that if Miss Critten dies this money reverts immediately to the private hospital at Pleasant Plains?"

"Precisely," said Hedges.

The doctor emptied his pipe and blew gently through the stem. "It will take a trust fund of almost a hundred thousand to earn an income of thirty-six hundred a year. Wouldn't you think so?"

"About that," said Hedges. "Securities are uncertain since the war. It's difficult to say."

Words about death were beating against Bonnie's ears—"if Miss Critten dies." Miss Critten didn't want to die. . . .

An attacker lurking in a vestibule. A shot from the woods. Yellow capsules that turned light brown. Mystery books that turned over.

"Are you interested in the Pleasant Plains Hospital, Doctor?" asked Duncan Maclain.

"He owns it," said Hedges abruptly. "Lock, stock, and barrel, to use a phrase."

"A rather unfortunate one, Hedges." Satterlee slapped one hand down with a bang. "It's a phrase that has to do with guns. You called the inspector's remark 'gratuitous' a short while ago. Yours is worse. I might take it you think I shot Fred Vreeland."

"I think I'd like Bonnie to show me over the Vreeland house," said Duncan Maclain. "I'll tie my dogs in the foyer." He stood up.

"Certainly, Captain Maclain."

Bonnie didn't want to play guide, but one couldn't be discourteous to a blind man. She wanted to stay, wanted to hear more of Satterlee and his hospital at Pleasant Plains that would get a hundred thousand dollars if Bonnie Critten should die.

Eyes followed them—speculative eyes, interested eyes, casual eyes, keen eyes—watching the captain's light touch on her arm, studying their progress into the dining-room.

"We go down here, Captain Maclain. The old kitchen is still in the basement and almost intact. Aunt Ludwina had a modern one installed next to the dining-room."

"I understand this house is very old, Bonnie."

She was watching with fascination the feather-light touches of his fingers on furniture and walls.

"It was built ten years after the Conference House, which is near here. That was built by Captain Billopp in 1679. He and old Pieter Vreeland were friends."

Maclain smiled. At the bottom of the stairs in the low-ceilinged, smoky-beamed kitchen, he touched a high-backed chair, pulled it out from the long table, and sat down.

"So this house dates from 1689?"

"Yes." Bonnie perched on the table edge beside him. "Captain Chris Billopp sailed his sloop, the *Bentley*, around Staten Island in three minutes less than twenty-four hours—so New York got the island instead of New Jersey. The Duke of York had ruled that New York owned all the islands in the bay that could be sailed around in less than a day."

"And Pieter Vreeland—" Maclain's sentient fingers drummed lightly on the table edge.

"I've heard he was with Captain Billopp." Bonnie laughed lightly. "I'm not guaranteeing how much of this is true. Billopp was granted a thousand acres of land. Later, Pieter Vreeland was granted some, too—near his friend. On September 11, 1776, Lord Howe met with Benjamin Franklin, John Adams, and Edward Rutledge at Billopp's house in an attempt to avoid the Revolutionary War."

"With about as much success as the attempts to avoid the one going on right now." The captain frowned. "Your history is interesting, Bonnie. It would be a shame to have the Vreeland mansion torn down."

"But Aunt Ludwina left it to De Frees because he promised to keep it intact. I heard her say so myself."

"It may not be up to De Frees—or anyone," said Duncan Maclain. "The fate of the Vreeland property, Bonnie, rests in the lap of Mars, the god of war." He took a cigarette case from his pocket, gave her one, and lit his own with such quick facility that Bonnie was unable to follow the guiding motion of his thumb along the paper cylinder.

"That's funny—" Bonnie slid from the table and found an old pewter candlestick to use for an ash tray. The captain reached for it unerringly. She couldn't help asking, "How did you know that was there?"

"I heard it when you set it down."

The grayish light from the high-set windows touched his eyes. For an instant, the illusion returned that he was watching her, reading her face, appraising the color of her eyes and hair. "What was funny, Bonnie? What did you start to say?"

"Nothing very important. Carl Raecke was interested in the fate of this house, that's all. He spoke of it last night. He's a friend."

"The shipbuilder?"

"Yes. Do you know him?"

"I've never met him." Smoke curled up about the captain's crisp, dark hair. "Davis mentioned that he rode part way out with you on the train and left rather hurriedly at the station before his own."

Bonnie snubbed out her cigarette, irritated that the police had been brought to mind again. She disliked being checked on. Next they'd be searching her rooms on Tenth Street.

"The old dungeon's over here," she said briskly. "It's used as a storeroom now. There's a legend that a passage led from it underground to a point near the shore. Do you want to go in?"

"Yes," said Maclain.

She clicked a light switch and opened the studded wooden door. He took her arm and let her lead him about the low, vaulted room. Occasionally he reached out quickly to rap with his knuckles on the thick brick wall.

"It smells delightfully of spice and preserves," he remarked when they stepped back into the kitchen. "But if any underground passage ever existed, it's well filled up now."

"I'd have found it when I was little," Bonnie admitted, and added, clinging to childish imagination, "still, it might have existed years ago." She opened another door. "This is our only authentic secret—a back staircase to the slave quarters on the top floor."

"Let's try it," Maclain suggested.

"It's dark," Bonnie warned, without thinking.

"It's never dark to me," said Duncan Maclain.

Bonnie took his hand and led him up in silence to the squeaky board by the door on the second floor. Idly she reached out and turned the knob.

"You're frightened, Bonnie." Maclain's strong fingers closed tighter on her hand.

"Yes," she said. "I am."

"More than you were last night," he continued. "What's wrong?"

"This door—it's been screwed up fast for years. But it opens now." She led him through it.

"Where are we?" His voice was very low.

"We're close to the guest room at the end of the second-floor hall." She stood quite still. "I slept here last night. Captain Maclain, I wish you'd come in a minute and sit down."

He followed without comment.

Bonnie said, "Listen, please." She returned to the stairway, stepped lightly on the squeaky board, and rejoined Maclain. "Did you hear anything?"

The captain crossed his long legs. "Perfectly—the loose board on the landing." He locked his hands behind his head. "You hear it last night, I suppose?"

"Yes." Bonnie moistened lips gone dry. She closed the bedroom door and sat down stiffly. "Why should anyone want to kill me, Captain Maclain? I asked that same question of my fiancé, Alan Thorne, last night. He came up right after you had gone."

"So there's been another attempt, has there?" The lines of the captain's mobile mouth grew hard. "I came out here to find the answer to your question. The shooting of your cousin last night rather spurred me on." His hands clasped until the sinewy backs turned white, then slowly flexed open. "At my suggestion. Inspector Davis talked this morning with Alan Thorne."

"With Alan? Why?"

"You met him at Fred Vreeland's, I believe."

"Who told you that?" Bonnie asked swiftly.

"The New York police are a strangely thorough and disconcertingly persistent body of men," said Duncan Maclain. "Once a law violation comes to their attention, they have a habit of digging into many angles. You suffered an attack by an unknown man in the darkened vestibule of your home."

"That had nothing to do with Alan."

The captain spread his hands in a gesture. "Mr. Thorne is auditor for your aunt's estate. From a quick survey of the books this morning he could find nothing wrong. He's giving them more time." Maclain touched his Braille watch. "We expect him out here later today."

"I don't like Alan dragged into this."

"The situation has altered since we talked last night, Bonnie." The captain's winning voice had its strong quality of reassurance turned full on. "You've become involved in a murder through no fault of your own. Incidents which might have been accidents before have now assumed serious proportions. The shot from the woods begins to look more deliberate. You started to tell me about something else. Suppose you go on."

It came in a flood, once she started: Her fear of another attack on New York's darkened streets. The subway and the impersonal, white-faced man. Carl Raecke's timely arrival and his sudden dash from the train. The step on the stairs. The capsule that changed color. The book that was turned over.

Maclain listened without interruption. When she told of finding Fred Vreeland, his hands unclasped. From that point on, his restless fingers were never still.

"Is the capsule box still on the table?" he asked when she had finished.

"Yes." Bonnie picked it up gingerly and slid back the cover. "Did you think it might be gone?"

"I think that such an obvious disappearance would be

most crude," said Duncan Maclain. "I judge from your silence that the capsules are once more yellow."

"They are." Bonnie hurriedly set the box back on the table.

"That seems to fit nicely." The captain pursed his lips, got up, and stretched. "Someone came in while you were in the bathroom and substituted the deadly brown for the harmless yellow. This morning, this clever person put the yellow pills back again."

"Who?"

"Undoubtedly the person who stepped on the creaking stair. Let's say someone who attacked you in your vestibule three weeks ago and robbed you to make attempted murder look like simple mugging."

Watching him, half mesmerized, Bonnie found his rugged features unreadably bland.

"Let's say someone who missed you with a shot from the woods last Saturday—someone who entered this room last night."

An inside coldness attacked her. "That would mean this someone had to be in this house last night and today, Captain Maclain."

"For a time, most certainly," said Duncan Maclain. "We have one great difficulty to contend with. There are several easy means of entering the house—a kitchen door, and long French windows in the dining-room. Any of them might admit a clever person to the use of that back staircase without being seen from the hall. That's why I asked you to show me around the Vreeland home."

"But you can't possibly believe—"

"I only believe what I know, Bonnie," said Duncan Maclain. "And I know that you were attacked both in New York and here. I know that your cousin was shot last night on the train. I know that I'm about to wangle an invitation to remain here in the house, and that a murderer is going to fail if murder is tried again. Meanwhile, suppose we take a look in your aunt's room down the hall."

He moved swiftly, opening the door for himself. Outside, he again accepted the guidance of Bonnie's arm. Voices trickled up the stairs. For the briefest of pauses the captain stopped her while he listened, then moved her on with a pressure of his fingers.

"Thirty-two." He whispered the number so softly in front of Aunt Ludwina's door that Bonnie wasn't sure she had heard it.

She asked him when they had gone inside and closed the door. "Did I hear you say 'thirty-two'?"

"You did." He was standing erect, his fine head slightly lifted, as though he might sense without seeing the layout of the room. "I live in a world of numbers, Bonnie—a world of numbers and sound. Numbers of paces between chairs and tables, numbers of paces in halls, numbers of steps up and down. Once I've been over a place, the numbers will guide me; I don't even need Schnucke to lead me around."

Bonnie couldn't help asking, "And what about the sound?"

"It gives me the size of this room, for instance," said Duncan Maclain. "It's large—approximately twenty by thirty. In addition, it tells me that it's furnished and that the draperies and upholstery are heavy. I can check, of course, if I take the trouble to feel my way around."

"That seems almost miraculous."

The captain smiled. "The skepticism in your voice betrays itself through sound. It's more than strange to me that people with eyes refuse to believe what they visually can see. I read tiny dots with my fingers. To you they would be but a blur. Some blind people can tell when they pass the house of a friend while walking on the street. They know the sound." He hesitated. "Two murderers are dead, Bonnie, because they refused to believe that I am an accurate shot at sound."

"You shoot a pistol at sound?"

"Ask Inspector Davis," said Maclain. "He can tell you how members of the Police Department loft squads in many great cities are trained to shoot in the dark—again at sound." His head moved a fraction to one side. "I'm wasting valuable time, Bonnie. We came to this room to look around."

"I can tell you anything you want to know about it," said Bonnie.

"I wonder," said Duncan Maclain.

Just then the door opened quietly, and Inspector Larry Davis came in. "They're serving sandwiches, Captain. I thought you might want to come down."

"I'm looking for poison," said Duncan Maclain.

"You never shake loose from a fixed idea, do you?" The inspector pinched the end of his nose. "Ludwina Vreeland died a natural death, Maclain. The autopsy report just came in to me by phone."

The captain walked to the window and stood looking out as though he might be studying Staten Island blanketed by the storm.

"My fixed idea is not that Mrs. Vreeland was murdered, Davis. My fixed idea is that where a patient dies of heart trouble we may find some easily accessible poison —strychnine, say—left about the sickroom." He stopped as if tired, and pressed the back of his hand to his forehead. "You might try the medicine cabinet in the bathroom."

"What have you uncovered now, Maclain?" Davis thrust out his jaw.

Without turning around, the captain swiftly sketched Bonnie's story of the book and the tiny tin box in her bedroom. He added to it the incident of the shot from the woods.

Davis listened, with a growing frown. When Maclain had finished, the officer turned to Bonnie and curtly asked, "Is all this true?"

"Of course," she told him, stung by his brusqueness.

"Do you think I dreamed it?"

"I wouldn't know," said Davis. He vanished into the bathroom. A clinking of bottles followed. The inspector returned and sat down.

"Well?" said Duncan Maclain.

"There's a box of strychnine sulphate powder, apparently for hypodermics. There's also a bottle of capsules. marked, 'One every three hours, or as needed.'"

"Light brown?" asked Maclain.

"Yes," Davis admitted unwillingly. "Light brown."

"It wouldn't be difficult for a potential poisoner to empty a few of those capsules of their innocent contents and substitute strychnine, would it?" The captain was speaking to the world outside, a world he would never see again. "If one wanted to kill someone on short notice, they'd be handy to have around."

"Let's get back to the dream department." Davis crossed his legs and viciously demolished a toothpick between his powerful teeth. "We have it on record that three weeks ago Miss Critten received a blow on the head that knocked her unconscious. What's the use of building more trouble, Maclain? Miss Critten admitted to you that the capsules in her room are okay today."

"Wait a minute, please." Bonnie rested her weight against the back of a heavy chair. "I want to tell you that I've quite recovered from the blow on my head, Inspector. I realize that this is just a pleasant game." Her sarcasm was deadly, smoldering with anger and fear. "By all means leave the strychnine in the bathroom. Dr. Satterlee might want to put some in my tea. Let him shoot me, as he shot Fred through the window of the train. Let him stab me in my sleep—" She broke off, almost sobbing.

Davis squinted at her cagily. "Why Satterlee?"

"Can you name anyone else who gets anything from killing Fred and me?" She left her post at the chair back and walked swiftly to the door. "I'm leaving for New

York right now. I don't intend to sit here doing nothing and let somebody quietly murder me."

"I'd advise against it, Bonnie." Maclain swung around at the window and rested himself against the sill. "Larry isn't always the most tactful man in the world. Besides that, he labors under the handicap of having eyes and being able to see. But he knows you're in danger as well as I do. He just dislikes admitting anything to me."

"I'm admitting nothing," said Davis with heat.

"Of course not, Larry." The captain smiled winningly. "Even on that point we agree. Still, I wouldn't leave for New York, Bonnie. Until a lot of facts become more clear, the chances are you'd never live to get there—any more than your cousin lived to get out here."

Davis, watching her keenly, made an attempt to smooth things over. "Maybe you need a sandwich, Miss Critten."

"I don't think I'll ever eat again. I have a headache. I'm going to my room and lie down." She slipped out before either of them could protest.

Something was going on downstairs. Bonnie heard De Frees's voice raised in cordial greetings. Curious, she took a few furtive steps down the main staircase to a spot where she could survey the lower hall. She came up quickly, conscious that another element had entered the scene to plague her. Carl Raecke had arrived.

A macabre sense of unreality accompanied her into her room. Nothing was real, not even Fred's killer now. The highboy in the corner, the old Dutch ship done in faded embroidery on a chair, the painting of skating scenes on a Rotterdam canal—they were props in a tragedy, spotted about to increase a stifling atmosphere.

Bonnie Critten wasn't real. The hard-headed inspector considered her a wraith-girl crazed by a knock on the head. He was cleverly passing his doubts along to the one man who believed her—Captain Duncan Maclain.

Well, Bonnie Critten was real enough and smart

enough to know something that none of them knew. Bullets came from a gun; guns used cartridges—and automatic pistols ejected cartridges after each shot.

A broken-down shack stood concealed in the woods near the junction of Craig Avenue and Hylan Boulevard. If there was an empty cartridge to be found in that shack, it would prove, at least, that she'd been fired upon the Saturday before. It would also prove that the bullet had come from an automatic. To thrust such an empty cartridge down the throat of the doubting-Thomas inspector might be fun.

Bonnie was getting crafty. Her furs and galoshes were in the closet downstairs. She had heard Maclain and Davis go down. She opened the door with caution, for she had no intention of facing the somber gathering in the general hall. Tiptoeing with care to cheat the sentinel ears of Captain Maclain, she went down the hall to Katherine's room.

A heavy cardigan was hanging in the closet there. Bonnie put it on and picked up a pair of knee-length, fur-topped boots from the closet floor. They were large, but not uncomfortable.

The board in the old back stairway creaked as she went down. Oroondates was in the modern kitchen when she started out of the back door.

"The snow's too deep, Miss Bonnie." He cocked his ancient head to one side and fixed her with one birdlike eye.

"I want to take a walk by myself, Oroondates. Please don't tell anyone I've gone."

"I'll say nothing, Miss Bonnie." He clucked unhappily. "But the snow's much too deep. You'll sure enough bog down."

Ten steps outside almost convinced her that Oroondates was right. She looked back toward the kitchen window. The old man was staring after her with quizzical doubt, noting her lumbering progress. His visible disapproval brought out a foolish streak of stubbornness which sent her plodding on.

A short cut from the back of the house led through ice-draped trees up a gentle slope to Craig Avenue. Once there, Bonnie felt as if she had walked out of the civilized world. That section of Tottenville was desolate enough in summer and peacetime. But then its monotony was broken by an occasional automobile speeding by. Today there was no sound or movement.

Road and sidewalks were leveled. The center of the road was marked by two darker lines where some bus had fought its way to a lonesome destination. Bonnie scuffed out to the wheel tracks and followed one, walking it with a circus performer's skill.

At Hylan Boulevard she halted. The bullet had come when she was walking here on the Saturday before.

Bonnie summoned her courage and left the road to plunge through whiplike trees, leaving behind her a shower of brushed-off snow. Thirty feet from the road she stopped, staring dismayed at a tangled heap of graying boards jutting up from the ground. Under the weight of ice and the force of last night's gale, the flimsy shack had collapsed.

She strained at the smallest of the icebound boards and moved it a foot to one side by what seemed like sheer will power. Then it stuck firmly. Quick inspection showed that it was nailed to another board. Her common sense told her that cartridge hunting in that pile of rubble would require the services of two strong men.

Trees crackled to the left.

Overladen branches broke that way sometimes, just as the shack had fallen when burdened down. Or a careless foot might splinter brittle boughs on the ground.

It was about to snow again. A few wet flakes wafted in from the bay and settled on her cheek. She looked up, to find that a heavy black cloud was hanging low, adding more gloom to the grayness of the day.

Her own deep footprints led her back to the boulévard. She stepped as lightly as a frightened fawn, but still her footsteps kept rousing gentle echoes.

Every cautious movement brought after it an imitating scuffle from the resonant woods—a scuffle timed to a nicety, a mocking scuffle with a fearful quality of humor about it, as if it might pass her and assume an entity of its own if she lingered a shade too long.

She burst from the trees, found the automobile track on Craig Avenue, and started to run—twenty paces, with pounding heart and burdened feet, before an ice clod tripped her and she stumbled and fell.

The mocking echoes were still. Bonnie knelt where she had fallen, breathing quickly. The whimsical wind stirred the spindly trees into unwilling motion. Another branch cracked sharply.

Snow crunched farther down Craig Avenue as skid chains caught at the icy crust. A long, black car rolled from the Vreeland driveway and seemed to pause.

Bonnie watched it with fascinated despair. It would turn toward town and leave her kneeling there. It would desert her flatly.

The limousine turned toward her, kicked up snow, and drew up beside her. Maclain's giant Negro chauffeur jumped out from behind the wheel. "You hurt, Mis' Critten?" He raised her to her feet.

"No," Bonnie managed to say.

"Help her in, Cappo," said Duncan Maclain from the back of the car.

She settled beside him. His very presence revivified and restored her.

"I was driving down to meet Alan Thorne," the captain explained. "I thought you might like to come along." The car swung around.

"I'd love it," said Bonnie. She began to talk quickly, an endless chain of prattle. "Did you know that Staten Island was called the 'Place of the Bad Woods' by the

Indians, Captain Maclain? It was sold for wampum, shirts, and guns."

"What happened, Bonnie?" he asked her without a change of expression.

"I just saw the man who was in the subway last night."

"Are you certain?"

"I couldn't miss," said Bonnie. She huddled closer to Maclain. "I'd know those flat, black eyes in a dead-white face anywhere. He's been following me this afternoon—in the woods along the road."

The captain moistened his lips. "How do you know?"

"I have good ears, too, Captain Maclain. Added to that, I saw him just now—after I got in the car with you. He stuck his head out from the trees just as we turned around."

"Careless of him, Bonnie. Very careless. So many little things hang on carelessness." He took cigarettes from a fitted case on the side of the car and gave her one, then touched his to an electric lighter's ruby glow.

"I think that man would have killed me, Captain, if you hadn't come along."

"I don't, Bonnie. I sent him after you."

"You? But he was following me last night."

"He's an FBI agent," said Duncan Maclain. "Last night he was following Carl Raecke—not you."

Bonnie stared at him. "Don't you think, Captain Maclain, that in all fairness to me—and possibly for my own safety—I'm entitled to know exactly what's going on?"

"Unquestionably." The captain settled back in his corner. "The United States Government has offered a contract to Carl Raecke to build more ships in a single yard than have ever been built before. The key to Raecke's new project is the Vreeland property, Bonnie. Carl Raecke must acquire it from De Frees before the contract goes through. You'll hear the details this evening."

"That's why this man—this agent—was following Carl?"

"Exactly," said Maclain. "In times like these the Government is ticklish about men they give their contracts to. I'm telling you things ahead of time, Bonnie—placing a lot of trust in you."

"I don't understand. All the property went to De Frees, not to me. I have nothing to do with it at all. Yet—".

"Murder needs a motive."

They were at the station now and Cappo was parking the car. Maclain touched his Braille watch. "We have ten minutes before Alan Thorne's train gets in. . . . You have to help yourself, Bonnie."

"How?"

"Inspector Davis is a fine policeman, but, like all of us, at times he goes dead wrong. He thinks that you're a temperamental, artistic girl, frightened by a real attack and by last night's experience. He can conjure up a dozen reasons for Fred Vreeland's murder—concrete reasons such as jilted women. He can't find any reason why anyone should want to kill both Fred and you."

"Suppose two different people were involved?" asked Bonnie. "Suppose someone wanted to—to poison me after Fred was killed."

Maclain snapped out, "Who?"

"The doctor," said Bonnie miserably. "He'd know about the strychnine for Aunt Ludwina's heart. He gets the money, with both of us gone. He gave me the sleeping-capsules, after all."

"Did you know that there was strychnine in the house?"

"Yes," Bonnie admitted.

"How?"

"I helped the nurse take care of Aunt Ludwina over a week-end while Katherine was away. Dr. Satterlee left typed instructions in case of emergency—that is, if anything happened while the nurse was asleep or gone for a while."

"That means anyone might know about the poison," said Maclain.

"But someone had to be in the house last night to change my sleeping-pills."

He asked another question: "How did you get out of the house today?"

"Down the old back stairs and out the back door."

"Quite," said Duncan Maclain. "I heard you, but nobody saw you from the front hall. Last night was a fine night for a murder, Bonnie. Every footprint, every tire track, every noise—except possibly a gunshot—was obliterated instantly by the storm."

"You think that Fred's killer might have gotten in without our knowing it?"

"If you're not mistaken, somebody used that back staircase," he told her shortly. "I'd give a great deal to know if wet footprints were left behind." He touched his watch again. "Illogical events offend me, Bonnie. I have no eyes to see distractions, and my existence depends on logic. Things must keep their place, or I'll trip over them and fall. The changing of those capsules is too damn' pat. They were changed while you were out of the room, but the idea was worked out before Fred Vreeland was killed."

"Then it's Satterlee," said Bonnie with angry conviction. "He gave me the capsules in the downstairs hall. He—"

She halted, a brand-new doubt racing through her brain.

"Jumping at anything in the dark is dangerous," said Duncan Maclain. His lips contracted briefly and relaxed again. "The world is full of patterns which control us—the route we take to work and home; the remedies we suggest to friends for colds and headaches; the seats we sit in, when possible, on a train. Observant people sometimes learn our habits and use them to our disadvantage."

"I've never taken sedatives, Captain Maclain. But Katherine—"

"Suggested it to Satterlee, perhaps?"

"Yes," said Bonnie. "She did."

"Many people might know she had a habit of suggesting them." He clenched his hands tightly about one knee. "The conductor admitted under questioning today that Fred Vreeland, when he could get it, always sat in the right-hand front seat of the Tottenville train. He was usually drunk and liked to put his feet up on the seat which ran at right angles, and sleep. In addition, he was less conspicuous to other passengers on the train."

"You mean—?" Bonnie began.

"I know what happened," Maclain broke in. "Whoever shot him knew where he usually sat, and, furthermore, knew he was on that train. You said a few minutes ago that you had nothing to do with the Vreeland property. I want to find out what the Vreeland property has to do with you—and your cousin Fred."

"I can't imagine," said Bonnie.

"Neither can I," said Duncan Maclain. "Now listen! Your aunt's will is dated three months ago. Hedges told me she made a change then. Were you out here around that time?"

She thought for an instant. "Why, yes. I was here the week-end she decided to change her will. She and Fred quarreled."

"What!" said Duncan Maclain, sitting up straight. "Tell me all about it—everything that happened."

Bonnie thought back, trying to remember all the details of that visit. Katherine had been away that week-end, and the nurse had taken a couple of hours off to rest. Fred and De Frees had agreed to look after their mother.

Aunt Ludwina had been particularly difficult that day, insisting querulously upon getting up for a while. De Frees, at last, had acceded, over Fred's protests. The men made her as comfortable as possible on the soft chaise longue, where she had started to quarrel with Fred.

Bonnie, taking a late afternoon tub in the hall bathroom close by, had uncomfortably heard it all. Aunt Ludwina had accused Fred of living an immoral life, and his temper had immediately flared. They had argued hotly, and De Frees's efforts to smooth things over had only succeeded in further enraging the stubborn old lady. Even Fred had turned on him, yelling at him to be quiet.

Bonnie had hurried from her bath and, clad in a dressing-gown, had knocked and gone in, knowing that her presence would quiet the family quarrel. Aunt Ludwina, her sunken eyes still bright with anger, told her she intended to change her will. She was transferring the Vreeland house from Fred to De Frees. She didn't intend to have the Vreeland heritage sold by a drunkard so that he'd have money to spend on his women.

Now, as Bonnie was telling this to Duncan Maclain, a sudden suspicion of De Frees flashed through her mind.

But that couldn't be! De Frees would never get angry enough to murder anyone. Anger was not a weapon to De Frees, secure in the skill of his persuasive tongue.

Then she realized, with relief, that De Frees, furthermore, had no motive. Fred's death hadn't benefited him at all. Neither would her own death. Only one man would profit now if Bonnie Critten should die. . . .

She realized that Maclain was talking: "Were the servants there during the quarrel? In the room, I mean?"

"No."

"Satterlee? The nurse? Anyone else?"

"No."

Maclain fell silent, obviously thinking deeply. Presently he sighed and said, "You'd better get up on the platform, Bonnie. I hear the train."

The fervency of Bonnie's kiss caused Alan Thorne to say, "Um-m! Is there something stimulating in the Staten Island air—or should we part for eighteen hours and meet again?" He took her arm and they started down the ramp.

"Now that you're here, Alan—I'm recovering from a scare."

"Hell, I don't wonder!" He squeezed her hand with firm reassurance. "This is a rotten mess. I'm taking you back to New York, where I can look after you."

"Could you have saved Fred Vreeland from being shot, Mr. Thorne? Even if you'd been right there?" Duncan Maclain fell in step beside them, attaching himself to Bonnie's other arm.

Bonnie said quickly, "Alan, this is Captain Duncan Maclain."

The two shook hands. Alan's acknowledgment was guarded but gracious. "I've heard of you, Captain Maclain. You've done some astonishing work in your line. Are you working on Fred's murder?"

"Not officially, Mr. Thorne." They got in the car, and it moved off smoothly. The captain settled back. "I'd like to repeat my question."

"Could I have saved Fred?"

"Yes."

"Nobody could have saved him, could they? He was shot from outside." Alan spoke with deliberation as though some weighty problem had been dumped on his desk demanding a quick solution.

"Exactly," said Maclain.

"Just what are you driving at, Captain?"

"Bonnie's in danger," the captain told him with a serious air.

"Of what?" Alan twined his fingers in Bonnie's and held tight.

"Death," said Maclain.

"Rot!" Alan's smile was worthy of a hardheaded C.P.A. "Who'd want to injure Bonnie?"

"Fred's murderer." The captain stretched his expensive shoes out before him and seemed to be contemplating a few particles of clinging snow. "Could you save her, Mr.

Thorne, if she were shot through the window of the train?"

"But—"

"There are no buts, Mr. Thorne," said Duncan Maclain. "I came out here today on two counts. My partner, Major Savage, who is now in Washington, happens to be overlooking the Government's interests in a deal for a new shipyard to be opened in Tottenville. He occasionally asks me to lend what assistance I can, knowing I enjoy the work."

Alan's hand gripped Bonnie's more tightly.

"Last night Bonnie asked my advice. Mention of the Vreeland name tied me into this more firmly. Complications arose—murder and threatened murder. I decided to come out here without delay."

"Somebody tried to poison me last night, Alan." Bonnie's voice was once more tight with strain.

"If you know this person—" Alan began.

"I'd call checkmate," said Maclain. "I have no eyes, Mr. Thorne. Possibly that's why I believe the statement of an attractive young woman, when so shrewd a man as Inspector Davis is inclined to doubt it."

"Bonnie's not a liar," Alan said angrily.

"I judge that from her voice and conduct, Mr. Thorne, not from the deceptive superficialities of personal appearance. That's how I became involved in this game. I have no magic sixth sense. Actually, I'm dependent on how well I've trained my remaining four—hearing, feeling, taste, and smell. All of them have had to be overdeveloped to take the place of the missing one."

Alan's hand relaxed on Bonnie's. She had a moment of quiet, internal self-justification. She was ready to place her life in this blind man's care without a qualm. It was pleasing to see that Alan, practical and ultraconservative, had also succumbed to the captain's magic spell.

"What do you want us to do?" asked Alan.

A muscle twitched lightly along the captain's brow.

"I'm playing blindfold chess. I have to remember the position of every piece—my own and my opponent's. At best, it's a difficult game. It's doubly difficult when there's a death's-head crowning your opponent's queen. I want Bonnie to stay out here tonight, and I want you to watch her every second. I have found a motive which may fit the killing of Fred Vreeland, and Bonnie, too. . . ."

To Bonnie, the arrival of Alan Thorne seemed to have divested the Vreeland house of a portion of its funereal pall. When they walked in, Katherine was serving sherry and Wilma had turned out a large selection of canapés. Oroondates was in his glory passing his wife's handiwork about the room.

The inspector broke off a conversation with Hedges to take the captain's coat and hang it up. Instead of following Bonnie and Alan into the room, Maclain stood near the foyer leaning against the doorjamb while Bonnie made introductions.

"Carl Raecke . . . Bruce Hedges . . . You've met Dr. Satterlee before . . . Inspector Davis . . ."

Alan took sherry from De Frees and led Bonnie off to a corner. Speculative lines showed above his thin, straight nose. "All this place needs is an organ to look like a cathedral at dawn!"

Hedges came up. He was dry-washing his hands, and his sensual mouth was opened a trifle. He had obviously passed up the sherry for something a little stronger. "So you're the lucky Alan Thorne! I envy you, my boy; I envy you. If I were a few years younger—"

Katherine sailed over. "We want you to make an announcement, Bruce. Come along." She raised eyebrows and shoulders behind the lawyer's back as though asking sympathy for a harassed hostess.

Bonnie's small, even teeth bit through a stuffed olive. "If he were a few years younger!"

Alan was watching the captain make his way unerringly toward them from across the room. "How the deuce does he know where he's going?"

Bonnie said, "Your voice has always had a pleasant, raspy sound."

Maclain came close to their settee, but didn't sit down. "Did either of you hear Cappo drive my car into the garage just now?"

"I wasn't paying any attention," said Alan.

"I'm sure I didn't." Bonnie looked up at him inquiringly. The captain was slightly disconcerting with his checkup of every sound. "The garage is some distance behind the house, on the hill. It's at least half a block down."

"I didn't hear it, either," said Duncan Maclain. He left them to occupy a small divan near Hedges' chair.

"That guy must be strong as an ox," Alan remarked.

A silence fell on the room. Hedges stood up, with his back to the fire, looking very serious and not too steady.

"I have an informal announcement to make," the lawyer said. His eyes settled on Raecke, who squirmed in his high-backed chair. "Mr. Raecke has arranged today to purchase this house and all of the Vreeland land from the legatee, De Frees Vreeland. The price has not yet been agreed on, but it will be more than a million."

Hedges pulled his stomach in and wet a thumb to make a gesture of counting money.

"That depends on my colleagues, of course," said Raecke, with a scowl.

De Frees spoke up, his irritation covered by his placating smoothness: "Suppose you keep to the point, Bruce."

"I am authorized to say this much," Hedges continued. "The Government is prepared to grant Mr. Raecke and his associates the largest contract for building ships that has been let out since Pearl Harbor. The Vreeland land is an ideal site for this proposed modern shipyard. I have no reason to doubt the patriotism of Mr. Vreeland or Mr.

Raecke. Consequently, I am confident this deal will go through. I think this will be a tremendous step forward in our defense efforts. . . . I'd like a word from Mr. Vreeland." Hedges left his post and sat down.

De Frees made a brief acknowledgment, closing with: "Any reasonable offer on Mr. Raecke's part will close this deal. My only stipulation is, as I said today, that in accordance with my mother's wishes this house is to be preserved in good condition."

"A million bucks!" Alan whispered in Bonnie's ear. "Six months ago this wolf-run out here wasn't worth a song. Do you cut in on that melon, Bonnie?"

She shook her head. "No, but we're not going to starve. I can paint what I want to now, Alan—thirty-six hundred a year."

Alan whistled softly. "I should jilt you for some honest working girl, but all I can think to say is, 'Kiss me, dear!' "

Bonnie pecked at his cheek, but was silent as Inspector Davis stepped into the room.

"I'm leaving in a minute," he said. "I just talked to Headquarters by phone. I hate to bring up this matter of Fred Vreeland's murder again, but I feel his relatives are entitled to know what we're doing."

De Frees stared into the fire. Hedges cleared his throat. Katherine examined a stocking seam. Raecke bit the end from a new cigar. Bonnie looked into Alan's dark eyes and found them inscrutable. Satterlee sneezed and blew his nose.

"Mr. Vreeland's murder seems unusually purposeless." The inspector might have employed the identical tone to say it was going to rain. "His mother died a natural death last night while he was lying dead on the train. An autopsy was performed on both bodies today."

Satterlee muttered, "I nearly got pneumonia on that platform last night." He sneezed again.

"We have interviewed many of Mr. Vreeland's friends

today, with the exception of Mr. Thorne." Davis glanced toward Alan. "All of them were definitely someplace else at the time of the shooting. It may reassure Mr. Thorne to know that we have checked with his office. He was on a late audit last night, working with five others at the time Fred Vreeland was shot."

Bonnie drew a long breath and let it out slowly.

Davis continued in almost monotone: "We drove a police car from Atlantic Station to the station at Tottenville. Someone might have shot Fred Vreeland at Atlantic Station and by breakneck driving have managed to be on the Tottenville platform to meet the train—about four miles. We doubt if the train could be beaten by a car in a run to Atlantic Station from Dongan Hills."

"Is that hitting at me, by any chance?" asked Raecke, removing his cigar.

"You hit at yourself by your own actions last night, Mr. Raecke." The inspector was coldly official. "Is it your usual habit to leave a young lady a station ahead of your own, and dash from a railway car?"

Raecke flushed darkly. "Until I got mixed up in this Vreeland land deal, my habits were usually nobody's business but my own. A man's been following me for the past six months. I saw him last night in the forward car and suddenly decided to duck him."

"For any particular reason?" asked Davis.

"Yes—a very particular reason." Raecke hesitated. "I made a late call on an old friend to give her news of her son's arrival on one of our ships. She lives between Old Town and Dongan Hills. Her husband's away. If it matters a damn to anyone, I didn't want a report going out that at two o'clock in the morning I was calling at her house. My precious shadow picked me up at Dongan Hills when I took a taxi home."

"I'd say that shadow cleared you, Raecke," said Satterlee through a sudden fit of coughing. "I'm the only one who could possibly benefit by Fred's death. De Frees has a million, Katherine a fortune, and Bonnie's fixed for life. I get a hundred grand as soon as I dope out another air-tight scheme to knock off Bonnie. You'd better keep an eye on me."

"Or maybe on Bonnie," said Duncan Maclain. "She wouldn't be fixed for life if Fred were alive—unless the will was misinterpreted by me."

Bruce Hedges hiccuped politely and said, "That's rather silly, isn't it?"

Raecke rose and consulted his watch. "I have to go."

"New York?" asked Davis.

The shipbuilder hesitated. "Yes."

"I came out in the police car," Davis told him. "I'll be glad to drive you to town."

"I can take three in my sedan," Satterlee said.

"Captain Maclain and Alan have promised to spend the night, so don't include them." Katherine pushed aside her untouched glass. "The funeral's tomorrow, and Captain Maclain has kindly offered the use of his car. We're most grateful." She and De Frees walked toward the foyer with Raecke and Satterlee, and stood chatting near the door as coats were put on.

The inspector looked up out of nowhere and took Bonnie's hand. "Do you still hate me?" He talked to Bonnie, but looked at Alan with a twinkle in one gray eye. "I was stinking to her this afternoon."

"She probably had it coming," said Alan.

Davis grinned. "I had to be mean or she'd have started to cry. I made her mad." He glanced over his shoulder and saw that no one was near them. "Don't worry, Miss Critten. You may not think so, but you're as safe as in church with Duncan Maclain and that devil Dreist guarding you. Various deluded gentlemen have been potting at him for twenty years. Most of them are dead. Maclain's still hanging around." He saluted airily, and was gone.

The front door closed. Cars moved off. That temporary

acute sense of emptiness and loss which follows the departure of guests pervaded the room.

Maclain got his dogs and settled himself by the fire. The animals lay quietly, heads on paws. Schnucke closed her eyes, lulled by a touch of her master's finger. Dreist eyed Katherine unblinkingly, holding her in the line of vision without moving his trowel-shaped head as she pulled a chair closer to the hearth.

De Frees came back to the mantel and stood there looking gray and worn. "What the hell am I going to do with a million?" He slid into a chair and stretched his shapely feet toward the flaming logs.

"What you don't need," said Katherine, arranging her already perfect hair, "you might split between Bonnie and me, now that Fred is gone. I doubt if Mother knew she was leaving you a million when she handed this property down."

"I'm sure I got much more than I expected," said Bonnie. "Actually, I expected nothing at all."

"That's what usually happens in the estates I've audited," Alan put in, and added as an afterthought, "Hedges seemed to be celebrating."

"Why shouldn't he?" asked De Frees. "He's administrator. This shipyard deal means one whale of a fee." He took note of his sister's careful work on her hair. "What's the matter, Kit? Are you sore?"

"Over getting a hundred thousand instead of a million?" Katherine laughed lightly, then left her seat and placed a light kiss on the bald spot starting above her brother's brow. "Why should I be sore? Money never meant anything to me."

De Frees reached up and seized her hand. "If you want me to split it, say so, Kit. I have plenty from my business. Get Hedges to draw up anything that suits you and I'll sign. Is that okay?"

"Do you mean that, De Frees?" Katherine covered her mouth with her hand, so that her expression was difficult to decipher.

"Certainly I mean it. You'd better take me up while I'm in the mood."

Katherine said, "I'll wait until you've had a chance to think it over."

A clatter sounded in the dining-room. Oroondates appeared, beating lustily on an old bronze dinner gong.

Maclain stretched. Bonnie had noticed that his eyes were closed and had decided he was dozing. He said, with a grin that brightened his whole face, "That certainly sounds good to me."

Bonnie wondered for a moment after they sat down at the table what the courtesies to a blind man should be. She dismissed her worry when she saw the captain locate his food with delicate touches of knife and fork. Five minutes later she had forgotten that the striking man on her right was unable to see.

Katherine served coffee in the hall. Later De Frees and Alan played gin rummy.

At nine, Cappo came in, bringing a box from the captain's car. He had been assigned to quarters over the garage. Maclain told the giant Negro that he wouldn't need him. Cappo bade them all good night, with an ivory grin.

The captain dumped the contents of the box—a fifty-piece jigsaw puzzle—on the surface of a table near the center of the hall. Slowly it began to shape under his sensory finger tips—two pieces hooked together, a third one found and added; four, five, six, and more.

De Frees and Alan quit their cards and came to watch, but Maclain was lost in his puzzle. His rugged features were deep with lines of concentration as he found the last segment and fitted it in.

Only then did he seem to be conscious of those about him. "I'm sorry if I've been rude," he said contritely.

Alan exhaled cigarette smoke with a noise approaching a sigh. "I can't do those things when I look at them."

"Working puzzles in darkness is a game of solitaire," said Duncan Maclain. "That's why I usually win."

"I'm going to bed," said Bonnie.

She was half asleep when Alan rapped on her door a few moments later. "Bonnie, I'm right across the hall, and Maclain's in the corner room. If you want anything just holler. Good night, darling."

"Good night, Alan."

A night to sleep. A cold night with ice scum on salt pools along the Kill.

A long time later Bonnie woke, to hear the noisy, whirring clock downstairs set itself with a preliminary grinding of gears and strike the hour of three.

Bonnie checked with her luminous wrist watch. If the clock was right it meant that Alan had said good night four hours before. Her watch and the clock agreed. She must have slept soundly.

A white, diaphanous object was moving at the window. The fire was dead. The object at the window kept fanning her gently, restoring the icy guest room to its original clammy chill.

Bonnie set her teeth and turned on the table lamp. A white curtain was billowing in, moved by a late night wind from over Arthur Kill.

She got up and closed the window. Outside, the night was clear and starry. The threatened snow of the afternoon had proved a false alarm. She put on her flannel dressing-gown and crawled into bed again.

She put out the light. Now the room was really black— black as the world must be to Duncan Maclain.

Bonnie shut her eyes and listened. The Vreeland house was silent—quiet as the grave except for a strange, persistent trickle.

Was Maclain awake, too? He lived by his ears and the touch of his marvelous fingers. Was he sleeping now? Or lying as still as Bonnie, and listening?

Three o'clock in the Vreeland house—and someone was

filling a bathtub at the end of the hall.

Certainly it was a comforting sound, not like the squeak on the stairs she had heard the night before, not like the echoing footfalls in the woods. A homely sound—water running slowly into the old-fashioned Vreeland tub. A sound she had heard a hundred times before. Surely, not the kind of sound that might terrorize a girl.

Yet something in the sound was wrong. Water usually rushed out from the nickel faucet, gushed with a roar when you turned it full on. Now it was trickling. Somebody was being very considerate. It would take everlastingly long to fill the tub at that rate.

It was probably Duncan Maclain. "It's never dark to me," he had said. Equally, it was never light; day or night were the same. Perhaps he took late baths to help him sleep.

Fingers were tapping on the door, and a voice said softly, "Bonnie!"

She switched the reading-lamp on, and then called, "Come in."

De Frees came in and closed the door behind him. His nonchalance instantly reassured her. "I was worried about you, Bonnie." He seated himself on the bed beside her. "Couldn't you sleep? I heard you shut your window."

"I was cold, I guess, and then I heard water running." She raised her hand. "Listen! You can hear it now."

He lit two cigarettes and gave her one. "That's what got me up. The fixtures must have frozen and started a leak." His even teeth showed in a grin. "This is a touch of old times, eh? It wasn't so long ago that Fred and I used your room for a smoking-room to dodge our suspicious mother."

"I remember it only too well, De Frees. One of you squatted on either side of the bed keeping me awake until dawn. Then I had ashes to clean up after you'd gone."

"Yes," he said absently. "The ashes. There are always ashes after people are gone."

"I'll miss Fred and Aunt Ludwina, De Frees."

"Sooner or later, Bon-bon, we all have to die." He shifted his position. "That blind man is turning tragedy into a circus, Bon-bon. Is there any necessity to keep him hanging around?"

"He decided to stay, himself. He's worried about me."

"Why?" The light shone on his forehead, deepening the shadows of his frown. "Surely not over that mugging that took place in town!"

Bonnie snuffed out her cigarette, and when she looked at him De Frees had moved closer. It was then that she saw, in the pocket of his dressing-gown, the deadly outline of a gun. And she knew the truth.

She tried to speak, but her throat was tight with terror and she got out only a whisper: "No, De Frees, not you!"

But she knew that it was. There was death in his face and there was death in his hand as he pulled out the gun, clubbing it in his fist. She was too frightened to move.

Then she saw De Frees stop short and get slowly to his feet, staring at the blind man and the dog called Dreist standing together inside the softly opened door.

"It will be easier to talk this over, Mr. Vreeland, if both of us sit down." Maclain reached a hand behind him and closed the door again.

There was a different type of death in the face of Duncan Maclain. His smile was cold as the pools along the Arthur Kill. It held De Frees, crushing his attempted speech.

"You had to be your brother's killer," Maclain went on. "Nobody else quite fitted—that is, once the motive was found." He seated himself in a high-backed chair near the door.

De Frees took a step toward him. Beside Maclain, the big dog growled very softly.

The captain said, "I think you'd better sit down."

De Frees took a chair beyond the bed in the shadows.

"That's better," the captain murmured. "Now let's go

over the ground. Three months ago you persuaded your mother to change her will—leaving you the house and land."

Bonnie gasped, and De Frees said, "That's a lie. I had nothing to do with it. Bonnie was there—at least, she overheard it all."

"That's the trouble," said Duncan Maclain. "Bonnie was there. It was very difficult in this planned double murder for a motive to be found. Then this afternoon Bonnie told me of the quarrel that preceded your mother's change of will. Bonnie said something that struck me as very curious. She told me that your efforts as peacemaker only infuriated your mother. Now, Mr. Vreeland, you are a very persuasive—I might even say smooth—talker. Isn't it odd that you didn't know how to handle your mother's temper? Isn't it more likely that you *did* know just how to handle it—that while you seemed to be soothing her you were very subtly making her more angry? *And Fred knew this.* He yelled at you to be quiet. He saw what you were doing."

"Why, yes," Bonnie said breathlessly. "I remember now. De Frees would try to excuse things Fred had done, and in doing that he'd just reveal more disgraceful things that his mother hadn't even known about before. Why—" She stared at her cousin in horror. "You were responsible for the quarrel. You started kidding Fred about one of his women, and then your mother had to know all about it, and when you told her she went into a rage. You plotted the whole thing!"

De Frees sat silent.

"Yes," said Maclain. "And I learned something from Raecke today, Mr. Vreeland." The captain's words rolled on, smooth and ponderous as some devasting glacier. "He mentioned that it was about three months ago when he told you there was a possibility of this government transaction going through."

"You're very smart," said De Frees.

"Sometimes I think so, too." The captain allowed himself a frown. "If either Fred or Bonnie talked about the quarrel and how you'd influenced your mother to leave you a cool million, that will wouldn't be worth the paper it's written on. 'Coercion' is the term, De Frees. Moral force applied to your mother to get her to change her will. You knew how shaky it was—to a point of offering your sister a share tonight to keep her satisfied. With Fred alive to testify, any court would set aside that will. And Bonnie at any moment might realize the real significance of that quarrel. Perhaps she had discussed it with Fred. At any rate, she could not be allowed to live. You've made two previous tries to kill her. One last Saturday here in the woods, another three weeks ago in town."

De Frees wet his lips. "And how am I supposed to have killed Fred?"

"You heard Katherine phone him to come," Maclain went on. "Probably on the extension phone, or maybe she told you. You sneaked from the house, taking a chance that your drunken brother would choose his regular seat on a late, uncrowded train. You shot him at Atlantic Station and drove back here easily, knowing that Bonnie and Satterlee would be detained by the killing at the station in Tottenville. The garage is far in back of the house—nobody was likely to hear your car go out or come in."

The captain sighed. "Then you tried to dispose of the second witness to your coercion by slipping Bonnie a poisoned pill. That might make it look like an accident, or like Satterlee, who would benefit by both deaths under the will. When that failed, still determined to make it accidental, you decided to knock her on the head just now and carry her down the hall. There you could stage a deplorable scene indicating that Bonnie had been in the bathtub and accidentally drowned." The captain put his hands on his knees and sat still.

"You're determined to make things messy, Maclain,"

De Frees said out of the shadows. "I don't intend to be done out of anything I'm already into so far."

"You've already made things messy," said Duncan Maclain. "Like most clever killers you're really stupid. You've made one bad error—hanging on to the murder gun which you hoped to plant on Satterlee sometime. My dog's uneasiness indicates that you might have it with you right now."

De Frees sprang up. "Well, take it, you blind-eyed fool!"

Light glinted against the automatic, but before De Frees could raise it, Dreist had jumped, clearing Bonnie and the high Dutch bed with the speed of a falling star.

De Frees shot twice, as Bonnie screamed, but tearing teeth were on his arm, shredding the dressing-gown, pulling the blazing pistol toward the floor.

The gun dropped with a thud from paralyzed fingers. Instantly the dog was loose, and diving in again. De Frees went down. The dog closed in a third time, searching for the throat.

"He'll kill him!" Bonnie found she was whimpering.

The captain snapped an order to the dog. "If you move, De Frees, the dog will tear you to pieces," he added just as Alan burst in from the hall.

"Bonnie!" Alan put his arms about her. She buried her face on his shoulder. She couldn't stand to see De Frees groveling under the dog that watched in such frightful silence unrelieved by any growl.

After a while they left, and Katherine was sitting beside her, and still she cried on Alan's shoulder.

The captain came back in. Straight and strong, he stood beside her for a moment, then reached out with his fingers and gently touched her hair. "He killed his brother, Bonnie, and would have killed you."

She'd forgotten that. Suddenly she sat up straight and dried her eyes. Life wasn't over, by a long shot. There'd be other things to see—beautiful things. Duncan Maclain would never see them, but still he didn't seem to care.

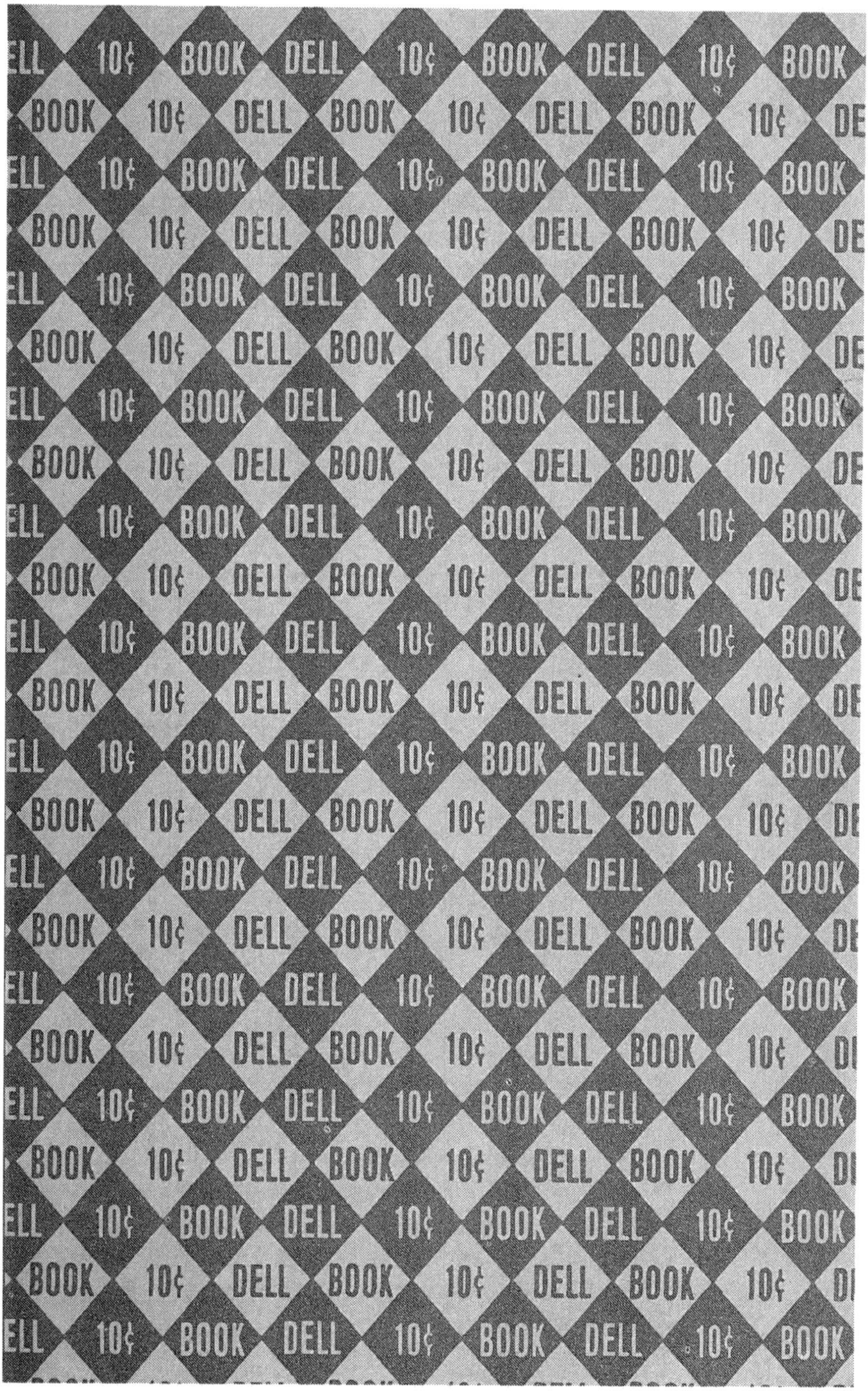
DELL
10¢
BOOK

CPSIA information can be obtained
at www.ICGtesting.com
Printed in the USA
BVHW051746260223
659247BV00008B/253